From Zero To One Hundred

Author: V.V. Hills

Dedications

Dadda

I dedicate this book to the man that I first loved, who first loved me, who showed me how to love and what real love is. I dedicate this book to Charles Burnette Sr., my father, my Dadda. He would have been so proud of me for doing this; as he was for my every accomplishment.

Dadda, now that you've gone on to be with the Lord, I feel an expectancy to continue on the legacy of what you have instilled within us. You always pointed out the scripture about leaving behind an inheritance for your children's children (Prov. 13:22). So, my aim is to teach them the Word of God and hard work ethic as you showed us through your lifestyle. I want them to understand agape love. You showed us how to love unconditionally. How to forgive; even when the situation seemed unforgivable (Mark 11:25). To love those who seemed "unloveable" (Matt. 5:44). Most of all, you showed us how to work through every issue until it was resolved. In doing so, we learned to never let the sun go down on our wrath (Eph. 4:26). You also taught us to keep God first in everything we do (Matt 6:33).

I could go on forever telling of the great man of God you grew into, but I will leave the rest for some of the testimonies I will tell. I want to sound off by stating that I love you more than I could have ever expressed.

Only God knows why I was not able to say my final goodbyes to you before you left this earth. Maybe He knew that I would've tried to move heaven and earth to have made you stay. Maybe He knew that my heart would have been so much more crushed; even though I feel like I would have been strong enough. I don't know. I do have some degree of peace in knowing that there was nothing left unsaid, no strife or anything that needed to be reconciled between us. Yet it doesn't erase the feelings of me missing my bear hugs and your prickly-faced kisses. I miss your goofy, backhanded compliments, your loud baritone voice bellowing through a room, you jumping in on our songs as an extra voice (even though you will not be singing with us) just because you want to be a part of our singing group so badly; knowing that you never remember all of the words to any songs. I definitely miss your corny jokes and your tacky outfits. Putting colors together that don't really go because "they're in the same family of colors". You fussing at my kids for petty reasons.

Man, life is so different without you. Your name comes up daily. Sometimes I still cry; I just do it in my private time. When the family is together, we constantly talk about how "I know Dadda would have loved this!" or " Dadda would have said that, if he would have seen or heard this or that."

What I hold in my heart most, that usually puts that stupid lump in my throat, is the thought of knowing, "he would have been so proud if he could see me right now (in certain moments)." Those are the times that I still have to hold back tears. Now, I know when Ma is proud. She will definitely say so. But you, you just had this way of showing your excitement that no one could ever duplicate. That's what makes me miss the way you displayed your proudness (my autocorrect came up, so I know that's not a word. But I like it).

I know you were not always the man we boast of you to now be, but this is who you became. For those that know him from his days of old, that's all that matters. He was a mighty God-fearing man and he made his family very proud. For that, he will forever be loved, honored, missed, and held to a standard that any other man in our lives must meet or exceed.

Momma

I also dedicate this to my Ma, Addie Burnette – GG. She is definitely the strongest woman I know. There has never been one whom has had my back (even to a fault) to the magnitude that this woman has. I love you, girl.

Despite all the adversity you have gone through, you have remained a pillar. For that, I admire you and pull strength from the mighty woman that I see in you.

You have been my friend and confidant. You have supported, encouraged, prayed, and ministered to me. I could go on forever, but I would never finish this book. Just know that there would be no Me without You.

I love you more than I could ever express in a lifetime. And as good as I am with words, I can not begin to describe my feelings for all that you mean to me. I think our relationship could be a book too. LOL. Becoming a wife and mother made me understand you so much more than I thought I did. And now that I am in your shoes and can truly see from your vantage point, I love, respect, and honor you so much more than I ever imagined I could. Thank you for every sacrifice. Thank you for your love. Thank you for your unwavering love. Just thank you, Ma. I love you and I will never love anyone as much as or the way I love you.

Big Sis

My next dedication goes to my oldest sister, Rhea McCarty. Thank you for just being you. You have been supportive, loving, honest, and just there. You are the friend that every sister and woman needs in their life. You know just how to whisk me away when it's time for a break from the stress of life, kids, whatever. We have cried together, laughed together, rejoiced together, argued, and made up. But that is what the bible says we should do (Romans12:15). You always jump in on what starts out as our crazy ventures. Even if you stay in the background, you make sure you do all you can to ensure that we are taken care of. I know you don't care for social media, but thank you for gracing us with your cameos so we can represent you every so often. I love you forever and always, sister. I know you don't like mushy, so I'm going to leave it at that. Just know that it is what it is and it's ALWAYS going to be. I love you always and forever.

The Poet

Now goes the thorn in my side, Charles Burnette Jr. LOL. I'm kidding. I love you, my one and only little brother. I have never met an individual with so much talent in one body and brain. I stand in awe of you, believe it or not. You have been the true epitome of the scripture (Deuteronomy 28:8) Let everything that I put my hands to prosper (in so many words). There has never been anything that I have seen you do, not be done with such excellence and perfection. Everything I have watched you do, I have done always to the point of envy. It always amazes me how you just jump from one gift to the other and leave the other behind as if you were not thee best at it. You can preach, rap, write lyrics at the drop of a dime, make and play music, play drums, cut hair, body build, teach health and wellness and make it sound interesting. I think you could probably be a comedian too because you can make people laugh with little to no effort. As Dadda would say, "Ya cold-blooded ya ol' joka!" I know we have our differences, but I love you, dude. You challenge me to be a better woman of God, I tell ya that! But I would not trade you for anyone else.

"The Law (as Dadda would say)"

Here goes the baby. I wish I could use an emoji right now to describe you. Just kidding. This dedication is for LaToya Z. Burnette, my baby sister. Now, I have to try and keep this short and to the point.

You have been my super rider. We sing together, we hang together and we do business together. In short, our lives virtually revolve around each other. But "how can two walk together except they agree (Amos 3:3)." Oddly enough, even if we don't agree, we always find a way to work it out so that we can still walk together.

I am so Godly proud of the woman you are. You are beautiful and will not allow anyone to make you waver in your walk with the Lord. I have told you so many times before how much I admire you.

Watching you lead praise teams; I'll back you up any day. Seeing the masterpieces that you create at the salon; I watch in amazement. And the way you have stood on the Word of God to push past what the doctors have constantly diagnosed you with; you are a walking living testimony of His Word (Isaiah 53:1-5). Watching you push past pain and sickness and worship your way out of what the devil wanted to make your deathbed. Man, you are a powerhouse! If people did not believe that God would do a mighty thing when you stand on His Word and trust Him, they definitely need to read your book (" WombBless

Woman" By LaToya Z. Burnette). That is another thing I am so proud of you for. You even wrote a book before I did. I showed you singing, makeup, doing hair, dressing up and you took hold of all of it and commanded the stage on everything! I could not be more proud as an older sister. I love you, Yo. I will leave it at that because what is understood does not have to be explained.

The G.O.A.T. (My Love)

Most of all, I want to dedicate this to my husband, Maurice D. Hills. You are my everything. We have literally grown up together (Proverbs 5:28) and it shows. You are my best friend, my confidant, my lover, MY superman, my everything. There has never been a thing I made mention of or a desire that I had that you didn't meet. You are something like Jesus in that way; doing the exceeding and abundantly above what I ask or think. I don't know what I would do without you.

Thank you for making my dreams come to life. Thank you for everything that you are and everything that you do. Thank you for supporting me through every venture and even jumping in just to prove that your support is genuine. Thank you for pushing me in those times when I wanted to throw in the towel. Thank you for being my shoulder to cry on. Thank you for embracing me with your loving and encouraging arms when I needed it. Thank you for the "just because" hugs. Thank you for loving me the way I need you to love me. Thank you for being everything I need you to be, and doing the work to find out what that meant (1 Peter 3:7). Thank you for the prayers in those times of not knowing what to say, but just knowing you needed to be there.

You may not be perfect, but you are definitely perfect for me. And I praise God for you, for us, and the life that He's allowed us to build despite our faults. And I can't forget to thank you for all of my babies (Genesis1:28). I mean, thank you for saying yes every time I wanted to "go again". LOL. I can't imagine our life without them; me not being a mom and you not being a dad. I feel like they are such a big part of our purpose in life. Look, babe! We are really doing this thing. I can honestly say that I still remember when I prayed for the things I have now. And you were the first prayer on that list. What I can say is that God definitely showed out.

    I didn't do everything right. So, I didn't know if all of this was out of reach for me. But to stand here with the love of my life after all these years, I still find it hard to believe that I'm not dreaming sometimes. If you ever wonder whether I love you or not, just know that I love you more every day that I live. After all we have been through and the more I know you, I love you more now than I loved you when we were in our "puppy love" stages. I love you more than when we first fell in love and everything was fresh and new. I love you more than I did when we first got married and I expected to spend the rest of my life with you. I love you more than I did each time I was fat and pregnant looking in your eyes, and you made me feel like I was the only and the most beautiful woman in the whole world. Today, I love you more than all of those moments put together and multiplied because we have endured the good, the bad, the ugly, and the "in-betweens", and we're still here to tell our story. After it all, you still chose me and I still chose you. Despite knowing your faults and you knowing mine, you still love me as you do. I love you, I'm in love with you and I fall in love with you more and more every day. Thank you for being all that I need. I love you ALL of it, babe

Momma's Babies

I would never allow an opportunity to go by without honoring my babies. So, Xavier (my only girl), Maurice II (my 1st boy), Maddox (my strong man), and MaZahn (Momma's baby), I love you to the moon and back a million lifetimes over. One of my greatest accomplishments in life is being a mother to you guys. You all give me a sense of pride that I could never explain and a joy that not even a lifetime will allow me to show you. To watch you all mature and grow into these beautiful beings and accomplish things that I never even thought to dream of, just makes my heart leap out of my chest. I know I embarrass you, but I can't help being so proud of what God entrusted to me. I know you guys laugh at how much you think I pray or the music I listen to, but I do it all to be the example for you that I want to see you manifest. Your jokes about me make me laugh, but they also make me feel good knowing that you notice. The bible says, "Her children rise up and call her blessed (Proverbs 31:28). You just don't know how it blesses me when you keep coming to me for prayer because you believe I have some special connection or relationship with God. As if He only answers my prayers because you have seen Him do the impossible. Trust me, it still amazes me too. You kids amaze me. I love you all and I look forward to all the goals you will continue to surpass. I will not do individual dedications to you because I know it will be too lengthy and emotional. Just know that "Mommy loves you all of it" and I always will. Everything I do is to please God and to make you all proud to call me your mom. I love y'all.

Introduction

To be honest, I am starting this with no knowledge of how this whole book writing process really works. All I know is that I promised my Father God that I would share my testimony with anyone who would listen. As I have strive to tell as many people as I can, I realize that it's a really long story. Sometimes there's just not enough time to sit with people and really tell them how good God is and what He's done for us. In addition, I knew that I could reach so many more people through a book. There are only so many people that I know or that I'll have an opportunity to speak with, but a book can go places I'll never reach. I've found that our testimony has already encouraged many of the hearts of the individuals that we've already had the privilege to share it with. It brought us such joy to see people light up and their faith become reignited after hearing our story. Those feelings of joy compelled me to write it out. I didn't know where to start; I just knew that I felt a consistent urge to just start writing and God would direct me on what to do once I got started.

This is what it's like walking with the Lord. There are times when you feel compelled in the pit of your stomach; that is the Holy Spirit urging you to do a thing. God doesn't usually give you a life plan from A-Z. He tells you in steps what to do and as you act in obedience, He'll reveal the next step and the next, and the next. He wants us to walk by faith and not by sight (2 Cor. 5:7). And just trust that as we put Him first, all of our other needs and heart's desires will be met (Matt 6:33). So, this book is a total leap of faith for me. I write this wondering will people want to read what I have to say? How far will it really go? Will it reach the masses or is it just for a few people to get that encouraging word in order to increase their faith? I guess I'll have to be obedient and see.

My Prayer For You

My prayer is for my book to be a blessing to all who touch it and take the time to read it.

Lord, I pray blessings over everyone that will share this book. I pray Your anointing on those that will embrace the words and apply them to their own lives as they strive to reach new levels in their relationship with You. Allow them to see manifestations of Your Word as they apply it to their daily lives.
In Jesus Name, Amen

Chapter 1: He Loved Me First

There is not a whole lot that I remember from my very young years of age, yet I know he was always there; Dadda. From the point of understanding, I always knew that he was a man that was all about family and he raised us as such. He was from Memphis, TN and my mom hailed from Chicago, IL. Yet, God made a way for them to find one another and leave the old lifestyles that would hold them captive to a life they no longer wanted for themselves and the family they intended to raise. I won't go into their life story because it would be a whirlwind of tales that I am not entitled to speak on; it is theirs to tell. But I just want to give little pieces of my dad that I think everyone should know.

There were things that I hated as a child or even as a young adult about our upbringing. Now that I have my own family, I see why and I appreciate the rules, the talks, and the "No's".

Dadda taught us to be givers. I always watched him give tithes and offerings at church (Malachi 3:10). When we were of age, he taught us the principles of it. Not only with money, but even by being a blessing to those around us (Luke 6:38 & Prov

19:17). I remember the first time that I showed generosity in giving. I don't remember the situation, I just remember Dadda coming to me in tears and giving me all the change in his pocket. I know that may sound like a small deed, but you had to know my dad back then. He used to keep his pants pockets full of silver change. His hands were huge compared to mine. I had to be about 7 years old or so. When he handed me an overflowing handful of silver change, as tears poured down his face, it moved me to the point of never forgetting how much it meant to give. In that instance, it was my earthly father, so can you imagine the heart of God? Can you imagine what He is doing in heaven when we give to each other or to the poor?

Another thing about Dadda, he definitely held fast to the Word when it came to not allowing the sun to go down on your wrath (Eph 4:26). He and mom would argue for hours when we were small kids. But when it was over, it was done. It was as if nothing had ever happened.

Raise Them With Realistic Understanding

Some people don't believe in their children seeing or hearing them bicker. To me, that's just not realistic and it hinders them from learning how to deal with life's issues. I have seen kids traumatized by something they see in public because they have never witnessed an argument at home. I've heard kids say that they felt like they were the reason for their parents' divorce. Because they never heard them argue and now they have to live with one parent or the other, they think one is upset with them. I strongly believe that as long as you keep boundaries of respect within your "intense fellowship", it will be healthy for the children and show them how to resolve issues when they are of age. Meaning, keep your voices at a reasonable level, do not call each other out of your names or use profanity. If you have to take a break from one another, make it known that you are solely taking some time to cool off and will come back to talk when heads are more level. And when you resolve the situation or issue, allow the kids to see that resolution. If they are not around to see the resolution, talk with them about it, so they can see the way issues should be handled. Of course, this is all based on the age and maturity of the child. Now, we all know things don't always work out this way. But if you act out of character in their presence, go back and apologize to them. Yes, apologize to the kids. Let them know that you realize that you didn't handle the situation properly and you want to ask their forgiveness for not being the example that you are called to be before them.

Showing them negative examples could either cause them to act out in rage, cause them to use the same behavior when they have issues, cause them to disrespect one parent or the other, or even build bitterness towards one parent or the other. The bible says do not provoke your children to wrath (Eph 6:4). That does not always mean that you have to directly offend them. There are things they could see or hear that could stir those feelings as well.

Hug, Kiss, Handshake

The same way he would have his conversations with mom was the same way he made us kids deal with our issues. No one goes to bed until all issues are resolved. Period. No matter how late that turned out to be, we stayed up until everyone was forgiven and all was forgotten. Tomorrow we will wake up and treat each other as if yesterday never happened. And you know what? It worked. We actually didn't pull the "all-nighters" until we got a little older. You know kids are resilient and it doesn't take much for us as kids to forgive. But as teens and young adults, it became a little tougher for us to work out disagreements without our parents' intervention. I don't remember when, but at some point during our youth, he started implementing this really funny thing that made us humble ourselves during this time of conflict. It was the infamous "hug, kiss, and a handshake"; I wish you could see how hard I am laughing as I write this. Dadda was so country that he thought of the craziest things. But you know what? It worked. No matter how mad we were, no matter how bad we wanted to hold on to that grudge, we could not help but burst into laughter every time it came to that part; the ol' " hug, kiss, and a handshake".

Now that we are all grown up, we will still resort to that method of resolution when we really want to show the other that we are sincerely being humble in our efforts of resolution. It's our way of breaking the ice and starting fresh. I even use it with my kids from time to time. Boy, Dadda really thought of something with that one. The bible says "and the greatest of these is love (1 Cor13:13).

Love

Dadda's biggest message was always love. He definitely sought to live by the scriptures, but this particular one, I would say, he actually stood on. He never held a grudge. He never stayed mad at anyone, no matter what they did. He was the epitome of what the bible tells us to do. If he was missing the mark in any area, it wasn't for lack of trying. Believe me, if he had a fault, he was working on it.

He had come to the place where he would get up in the middle of our visits because he felt compelled to pray. I would come to visit and mom would "shush" us as we walked through the door because he was spending time with the Lord. He would no longer watch anything with swear words or anything that entertained any lusts of the flesh or his flesh (Gal 5:16). And even if we didn't think it was so bad, if it was too much for where he was in his walk with God, we couldn't watch it either. Not around him anyway. Needless to say, that left us with very few options when he was around. So, we would have to sneak and watch some of our "guilty pleasure" shows while he was out of the house. Nothing too bad. Mostly reality shows. Don't judge me! LOL. The only thing is, he hardly went anywhere!

Family First

He was such a family man that he hardly went anywhere unless he was with us. He had few friends; we were his friends. Our friends were his friends. LOL. He was something else. He just felt that the world didn't have much to offer, I guess. I think initially it was because he and mom moved to Michigan by themselves and didn't have anyone they trusted except each other. After that, it was a matter of raising us kids. He absolutely had a stance on both parents being involved in that process. I'm sure mom wouldn't have had it any other way even if he felt otherwise. During our middle school and into the beginning of our high school years, my parents ended up becoming teen pastors at our church. I would say that kept us close for obvious reasons. We would have kids from church visiting our home all the time; going on outings and all that, so that kept us close to each other during that stage in life. Them working in the teen ministry phased out as we were starting to graduate from high school and move into the real world.

Skipping over all the details, we grew up, but we never lost our relationship with our parents. They always knew how to be relatable and make themselves available to us. Because of that, we were now adults with adult friends and our adult friends were also our parents' friends. We had cool parents that people could get advice from. Our parents were the ones that allowed our friends to move in because they didn't have anywhere to go. Our friends would actually call my mom and we did not even know about it. Just amazing. But in all of that, they always led them and counseled them according to scripture. When our friends stayed the night or moved in, they had to sit in on family prayer and go to church on Sunday and Wednesday nights. There were no exceptions or rule changes for friends. They were treated like family in every way. As crazy as that may sound to some people, it never scared anyone off. They always stayed or came back.

Raise Them Up

That was a very small picture of my foundation. Of course, there was so much more; good and bad. All in all, we were a fairly normal family for the most part. The core of it all was to put God first. We were taught to watch our words; don't say things that would give place to the enemy (Eph. 4:27). Meaning, don't say things that you don't want to happen because your words have power. Don't talk bad about others. Now, that's something God has not yet manifested His finished work in me. But I am a work in progress. We were also taught that when you do something wrong, repent. Concerning our health or any other issue; we were taught to pray, believe what the Bible says about our healing, believe that God has already done it, speak that we are healed until we see it manifested, and praise Him like it's already done. And we do all of this, despite a doctor's report because, we shall believe the report of the Lord (Isaiah 53:1). It doesn't mean that we don't take certain medications or follow certain orders given by our doctors. But as you take your medication, confess healing over that issue. God will meet you where you are. It doesn't mean you aren't walking in faith. You are simply using wisdom. If your body has gotten to the point of needing medication, a procedure, or surgery, you do what is best for you. Listen to wise counsel and what the Holy Spirit is instructing you to do. Do not act or respond out of fear and decide you want to "walk in faith" all of a sudden. Again, use wisdom. When the time comes and you are asked what is wrong? Or what is your ailment? You answer like this, "the doctors have diagnosed me with blah blah blah, but I am healed or I am asking for prayer against that report. I want the doctor's report to line up with the report of the Lord." And even if you don't say the whole thing, just be sure that your wording is always carefully worded to say "the doctors diagnosed me with or the doctors said this or that". Never take on the confession of saying "I have high blood pressure" or "I'm a diabetic". If you're sitting in your appointment and that doctor says, "you're a diabetic, right?" Your response should be, "Dr. (Such n such) diagnosed me with it (however many) years ago." That way, you're still not confessing that condition onto yourself. How can you truly expect to receive healing from something that you continue to profess that you have?

Let me also tell you this, God breathed His breath into Adam. That's why everything you say has power. That's why people, who aren't believers, can post and speak confessions over themselves and they still come true. God's breath is that powerful. It went into one man and that was enough for all of mankind to live from and speak from. When I say speak, I mean to use authority, to speak things into existence, and most of all. "Speak those things that be not as though they were (Romans 4 :17). " It's how we walk in faith. Faith is believing that we receive, before we see, feel, taste, touch, or smell it!

Faith is what brought me to where we are going in this book.

Chapter 2: Covid

I know, I know. Everybody is so over it, when it comes to hearing and talking about Covid. But this virus came through and changed life as we knew it for so many of us. Many of us caught the virus and got over it. We continued on with life as usual. Others were exposed and succumbed to it.

Before all of this happened there was some good for us. The virus was unfamiliar and spreading fast. Doctors, specialists, scientists, and government officials didn't know what to do. So, they decided to just shut down the United States. Most of the world had done the same; some took more extreme measures. Most of the country only allowed what they considered to be essential businesses to remain open. That meant my sister and I had to shut down our beauty salon. For us, it was a blessing within a curse because although we were receiving a break from work, we still had bills to pay. What do we do now? I called all of my debtors and advised them that I was one of the businesses required to shut down and that I wouldn't be able to make payments until further notice. Of course, that didn't fly. Most companies gave me something like a three-month forbearance. But before I could miss a beat, here comes God! Hey! The government decided to issue unemployment to those of us being forced out of or off of our jobs. The "big deal" about us receiving unemployment was the fact that it wasn't something they usually issued to people who are self-employed. So, now you can understand where the praise comes from. I wish you could have seen me shout and dance to hearing that news. Boy, was that an answered prayer! I didn't have to stop paying any of my bills. So, I didn't! Yes, I kept paying my bills! Then, believe it or not, we received a notification from our mortgage company that our auto-pay would stop because the government was allowing homeowners a grace period, from payment, due to the pandemic. They understood that many people were struggling and could not make their payments. Well, my husband's job was still considered essential, so he worked from home. His income had not stopped. (I'm going somewhere, people. Just stay with me). So, receiving this notification about not paying the mortgage didn't register in his spirit (remember what I told you in the beginning about listening to the Holy Spirit when you feel a strong feeling about something)? So, my husband began reading into the fine print. Come to find out, we could go without paying our mortgage for six whole months! Sounds great, right? Wrong! After the six months ended, you would be left to pay the lump sum of the payments missed. Now, if that ain't a slap in the face, I don't know what is. So, obviously, we opted to continue paying, which turned out to be a lengthy process to work out for some reason. It was like they were trying to make it hard to continue paying. Many people did not see the fine print or the pandemic caused such a loss in income for them that there was no other option for them. Despite the programs, unemployment, and many other ways the government tried to issue help, people lost their homes. Somehow, throughout this time, a grant program came up for small businesses, so I applied for it.

Unemployment

When I say I received unemployment, I mean I was comfortable enough to pay my bills and take care of a few extra things. And that's what I did. I continued to pay my bills. I even doubled up on a few of them. Things were going so well, I decided to clean up my credit. After I cleared whatever was listed on my credit report, I surprised my husband and cleared up his credit too. I used the extra money to get a leg up in this game of life. I didn't splurge it away just to look back and have nothing to show for it in the end.

In the meantime, all of us are home all day, just looking at each other. I can't go to work, my husband works from home, and my three boys are doing virtual schooling. My daughter had her own place. Our home has four bedrooms with one bathroom. Every woman reading this should have caught on. I mean, you should either be crying for me or laughing at what you know I had to be dealing with by living with a house full of guys and only one bathroom. It was complete mayhem.

Chapter 3: Time With God

But being in the house all of this time, I now have time to reflect on the fact that I have so much idle time on my hands. Once again, the Holy Spirit began to speak to my heart. He's telling me how I now have plenty of time and no more excuses for not spending time with Him. And you know what? He was so right. The movie " War Room" instantly came to mind. I wasn't battling the same issues she was in the movie, but I had some things to talk to God about. I had some things that I needed Him to fix in me. There were things that had to be shaken up and removed, restored, and revealed.

I had grown up in church and been a believer or Christian for as long as I could remember. But I didn't really have my own relationship with the Lord. Growing up, I always relied on my parents to lead us in our walk with Christ. They made sure we went to church. They made sure we read our bibles and prayed. So, am I really "saved?" Yes, I definitely confessed Jesus to be my Lord and Savior; but everything I did concerning Him, was it because of the family tradition or lifestyle I was being raised under or was it because I knew Him for myself and wanted that relationship with Him? I knew all about God, but did I know Him?

Now, I am still being delivered from the spirit of forgetfulness (LOL), so I am not one to verbally quote scripture and verses. But I do know the Word and I usually know when the Lord is speaking to me.

    Anyway, we are living in a nine hundred and something square foot house, right around the corner from both of our families (which we are both very close to). This was the home that my husband let me pick out right before we got married. It was just for him, our baby girl, and me. It was more than enough at the time. Until we decided to grow our little family into a big family (there was just too much love between us to keep it all to ourselves). So, we kept having babies!

Prayer Closet

After watching "War Room", I decided that I wanted my own sacred place to pray and spend time with the Lord. So, in the basement of our little home, there was this small cedar closet. It was probably 3' by 5'. I don't really know my measurements; all I know is that it was small. I could fit my vanity stool in it and I still had some of my clothes hanging on one side of me. My husband got me a few little gadget night light things to put in it and I even had him drill me in a little wire basket for my cell phone. At one point I allowed that closet to be junky. But once I decided that I wanted a war room, I cleared it all out. I wanted my own sacred space.

I tried using my bedroom for that purpose a few times, but every time I was entering the Holy of Holies, someone would bust open my door! Sometimes I would get an "oops, sorry" and sometimes I would get the " mom, can I ...?"

But when I tell you that something changed about that war room, baby, let me tell you something. I would tell them that I was going to pray or sometimes I would just disappear (they would know where I was). No matter how long I was there, who called, or who came to the door, no one would bother my time with the Lord. Sometimes I would be there for two hours. Other times I may spend thirty minutes. But it was my time with my Heavenly Father and I loved every minute. It went from once in the morning, to twice a day. My second time would be before bed. If something upset me during the day, I would go right to my prayer closet until I felt a release and peace to return to life.

But listen, He never gets tired of hearing from His children. As much as we want to talk to Him, He wants to hear from us and He wants to talk to us too. So, don't forget to take a few minutes to be still after you pray. Sit in silence and wait and listen for His voice. There will be times that He will drop something down on the inside of you. Other times, you may not hear or feel anything. But maybe later on in the day, you'll get a feeling or a strong urge to do something. Because you've shown Him that your heart is open to hearing from Him, He will speak to you. And because He is a Father, He will meet you where you are. Meaning, He'll usually minister or speak to you in a way that you understand.

For, at least, a month I would just weep in God's presence. To be honest, I don't even think I knew what I was really crying about. I guess I just felt a peace that for the first time, I was finally close to Him on my own. I had finally reached some degree of maturity to where I could connect to Him consistently like I had seen so many others do. It was a relationship that I always envied and wanted to have, but never really knew where to start or maybe I just didn't have the discipline to achieve it.

I had hours of worship music downloaded onto my phone. Sometimes I would just sing, other times I would pray.

Then there would be times that I would do a little of both. Whatever the Holy Spirit led me to do was how I spent my time. I would use headphones to block out any noises. Our house was, what I like to call, cozy. So, it was very easy to hear what was going on; especially with three young boys. So, having headphones made me feel like I was in a world with only me and my Father.

Chapter 4: Preparation

So, remember that we have unemployment money and all this free time with everyone sitting around the house, right? Finally, summer comes along. We have a fenced-in backyard lined with chopped wood from trees that had been cut down the year before. To burn it all, I decided that we should build a fire pit rather than buy another one that would just rot out. So, that's just what my amazing husband did! After that, I figured it would be nice to have some rustic benches to sit around the pit. So, I looked up some stuff on Pinterest and found this really neat and simple idea using cinder blocks and four-by-fours. It turned out awesome.

    My husband is amazing with his hands (Dadda called him "the jack of all trades and the master of many." I don't know what he can't do. And if he can't do it, he will watch some YouTube videos and figure it out). He truly makes my heart leap.

    Anyway, after building the bench, we bedded the area with rocks and added patio furniture, and the list goes on. Basically, it turned into an oasis. As we finished the backyard, my husband decided he wanted to put down new flooring in the kitchen. Well, as that began to turn into a small kitchen renovation, my mom had a prophetic Word for us. Out of the blue, my mom tells us that the Lord said, "It's time for y'all to move." Although we have motivation behind the updates we're doing in the house, we now need to search for a realtor.

She Was Who God Said Yes To

I saw a post on Facebook from a particular realtor who had just sold a home to Pastors Mark and Jackie Baldwin (Advancing God's Kingdom). This realtor stated how she has prayed with some of her previous clients, but she had never taken communion with any of them before working with this particular couple. That stood out to me.

We had just become acquainted with The Baldwins (who are now our pastors). But before that was the case, my mom was vouching for me to work with this realtor because of our new found friendship. I was apprehensive because I wanted to hear from God for myself on this one. I was going to be launching out into the deep. After all the time I had been spending with the Lord, I knew deep down that this was going to need to be a decision I made based on what God told me to do. I couldn't base this decision on the faith of my parents like I had done in times past.

Here is where the Holy Spirit comes into play, once again. I began to focus my prayers on who we should use as a realtor. Why was it such a big deal? Well, what I didn't say was, God had increased my faith. In my time of prayer, I had been praying about a new home (before mom had even given us that Word). So, I knew it was God using her when she spoke prophetically to us. She had no idea what I had been seeking the Lord about. The updates we were making to our home had not been in preparation to move (so we thought), we just wanted to make our cozy home more comfortable for us. We had always done that. Whenever we started to feel the desire to move or felt irritated with our living circumstances, we would paint, move furniture around, or whatever. Sometimes, we would repurpose a whole room. Those small changes made the whole house feel like a new home all over again for us. It gave us a settling and peace as we continued to pray and wait on the Lord to give us the "go ahead" to move on to our next home.

But, now we have the motivation and a timeline. The backyard was completed to our hearts' content and the kitchen was almost done just as it was time for us to reach out to a realtor. We had worked with a realtor previously. She was awesome, motivated, and worked with us right where we were. We truly loved working with her, but I was warring with the thought of going with what was familiar or launching into the deep with this new lady whom I had seen boldly professing and proclaiming her faith. She didn't just promote herself after making a sale. She actually gave what believers call testimonials of the sales that she made. Although it sounds like an easy choice now; at the time, I was struggling with the question of "how big has my faith really grown?" Should I just use my faith as I work with whichever realtor we choose? Should I listen to my mom's advice and go with the realtor she suggests since she is the one who prophesied to us about moving in the first place? All of this was swirling around in my head. My husband was leaving the decision to me because I said I wanted to pray about it. But as far as he was concerned, why was it taking me so long to hear from God about something so simple?

I had not yet opened up to him on my concerns nor was he aware of how big I was believing this time around. The reason I had not yet shared with him, was because my husband is a realist. He is such a provider that he looks at the obvious and makes logical and practical decisions. Which is what he should do when it comes to daily life and taking care of a family. You get up and go to work, bring home a check and pay bills. If that's not enough, you acquire an additional source of income. Do what you have to do to provide for your family. I mean, that is just the practical way of living that we all abide by; and he has always done that. He always makes sure that our family is taken care of and that we never go without. He loves me so much that if I ask for anything, he will do whatever it takes to get it for me. Because I know that, I am very careful in expressing my desires to him. I'm particular in which times to let him know, "this is between me and God. I don't want you to intervene. I am only telling you, so you can be a witness to Him answering my prayer." After saying that, he will back down and allow me to walk out my faith process. My point is to take the pressure off of him and allow him the peace of knowing that it's all in God's hands.

  In knowing the dynamic of our relationship, I wanted to make sure that what I was praying for was going to work out under God's plan and not by the sweat of my husband's struggle to make it happen. So, I chose not to tell him right away. A few weeks went by, of course, my husband started to get a little impatient with me. I should have just told him, but I guess there was some degree of fear there. Like, would he have the same crazy faith as me or would he shut me down and tell me to be realistic? I mean, he is the provider of our home.

Either way, I finally settled on launching out into the deep. Let's go with the new lady; Rochelle Ridgell. The first time we spoke on the phone my husband was not with me. This was my time to introduce myself and explain my expectations. And that's what I did. I told her how I had seen her testimonials on Facebook and could tell she was a woman of God. She confirmed. I went on to explain how we had been in our home for almost 18 years and felt that it was time for us to move on. Now, I can not quite remember if I told her over the phone or when she came to visit our home, but I informed her that after all this time, we were now ready to step out in faith. I said, " I am believing God for something big and I want a believer that's going to work with us in doing that." That was all she needed to hear. She got excited and started talking all about walking with the Lord and stepping out in faith. From that point forward, we prayed together and everything. She took the leap of faith with us.

Chapter 5: Harvest Time

Now that we have a realtor, we feel the crunch to complete our home renovations. The next thing on the to-do list is the bathroom. Remember we only have one bathroom. But it's fairly small, so whatever we do shouldn't take long. In the meantime, God is doing all kinds of awesome things behind the scenes.

Let me say this, when God is doing a new thing, it won't always be comfortable. And believe me, it surely was not. Doing any type of renovations, especially in a home the size of ours, was extremely uncomfortable. While my husband had the kitchen torn apart, everything from the kitchen was in the living room; the only living room. The kitchen and living room were central to the house. That's how we got to and from the bathroom and bedrooms. It was now cluttered with kitchen furniture and appliances. All the food we ate had to be microwaved or air-fried and eaten off of paper plates with plastic utensils. In addition to all of that, we were decluttering and cleaning out bedrooms in preparation to paint. It was complete chaos climbing over things going in and out of the house or back and forth to the bathroom. When he had to work in the bathroom, that was the most irritating. All I could do was praise God to keep from complaining. Working around one bathroom in the midst of it being renovated had to be the most trying thing ever. I'll just say this, I know I'm a child of God after being able to go through that! Praise God that He has gifted my husband to the capacity in which He has; he is very skilled for one who has not been professionally trained. He worked fairly quickly for someone who had to do all of what he accomplished, by himself. I love that man of mine.

Approximately a year and a half prior to this time, my husband applied for the student loan forgiveness program. They gave him the runaround and he had not heard anything back from them. Now that we are in the pandemic, we definitely aren't thinking about that. But while I'm having my prayer time, the door snatches open and my husband is standing before me with tears in his eyes just praising God as he hands me a letter stating that his student loan has been forgiven. I just started praising with him as he closed my door. God, wow. After all this time, why now? But then, I come out of prayer and get a phone call from an unknown number. I usually don't answer those, but I don't owe anybody any money, so why not? I am being contacted by someone from a grant organization. Remember when I mentioned applying for a grant concerning my hair salon? Since then, it had been about a month ago that I had been waiting for a response. They called to let me know that I had not responded to their email and I needed to do so in order for them to proceed with processing my application. I hang up and check my email just to find out that I actually missed the deadline. The email stated that if you did not respond by the deadline, they would move on to the next candidate. I was supposed to respond the day before. Knowing this, if they are contacting me after the deadline, I definitely have the grant! I hang up and start crying immediately. My husband panics asking me what happened. I can barely get the words out: We got the $10,000 grant for the salon! All within an hour or so, my husband found out that he was relieved from owing thousands of dollars to student loans. Right after that, I find out I'm receiving $10,000 to take care of my salon in the middle of a pandemic! God is good all the time, and all the time, God is good.

All while we are getting the house prepared for moving and being put on the market, so many things happened. God's favor had taken place in such crazy ways to the extent that we just knew this was our season of harvest. While going through old mail and paperwork, we found a check for a couple hundred dollars that we were still able to cash. In addition to my husband getting his student loan debt canceled, they ended up sending him a check for a few thousand dollars for overpayment (because he had been making payments on his student loan before and during the request for the write-off). God was simply showing out in our lives. I mean, there were still long periods of time passing, but considering the amount of time we had been in our home, it wasn't that long. I only feel that way now that I look back. At that moment, I felt so anxious. I knew better than that. The bible says, " be anxious for nothing, but in everything by prayer and supplication, with thanksgiving, let your requests be made known to God; and the peace of God, which surpasses all understanding will guard your hearts and minds through Christ Jesus (Phil 4:6-8)."

In my time of prayer, I had to constantly pray for peace and patience over myself. I was supposed to be trusting God through this process. If He brought us this far, why would He not follow through.

Trust and not Doubt

To be honest, I held on to this little inkling of doubt because the things I saw as a "big deal," never seemed to work out the way I would pray for them to. Not to say that I wasn't appreciative of all that I had. But there were some things in my life that I prayed and fasted for that just seemed to either fall short or not work out at all. Yes, I have an awesome husband and beautiful, healthy children. I even ended up with my own business. But I always felt that everything I achieved was on a smaller level than those around me. The way I saw it, we still hadn't "made it," you know what I mean? Nothing to complain about, enough to praise Him for, but not quite enough to feel like I could stand in a room full of bosses and talk about myself.

I know some of you will read this and think it sounds ungrateful, but there are many of you who will completely get it. I always felt like I was just one moment away from my "big break" in whatever I was involved in. It wasn't as if I wasn't being patient. Everything I held on to and thought was on its way to something bigger; I was involved with it for numerous years. Maybe, a decade at a time. I, along with my siblings, had met all the right people (so we were told). We did everything we were instructed to do. We had even received prophetic words that spoke into what we were doing and what would happen. A lot of it came to life, but in the end, it fell short. Right when it seemed like it should happen, it just wouldn't.

I know this may seem insignificant, but I want the person reading this to know that they aren't alone. Hang in there. I'm going to jump ahead of myself and tell you a little bit of the ending. God does answer prayers. He answered my prayers. It didn't happen when I wanted or when I thought He should. His Word came into manifestation when He had everything lined up.

I had to show patience and integrity during the wait. I had to be grateful and praise Him in the midst of where I was and what I was going through. There were changes in me that needed to take place. You know what? I was praying for a big thing. There were a lot of things that needed to be in position for that to happen. Other people's lives were connected to my blessing. Now when I pray, I think of those things. But I also know to pray about those other factors as I wait.

The bible says the race is not given to the swift or the strong, but to those that will endure it until the end (Ecc 9:11).

Chapter 6: Time To Sell

Ok, I may skip around, just stay with me as I remember all the pieces to this testimony. So, let's move on to selling the house. As we complete the finishing touches, Rochelle comes over and sits down with us. After we talk a minute, she takes a final walkthrough and tells us when the photographer will be by to do pictures for the website. I wondered why she never mentions anything about doing an open house or anything. So, I ask. You have to know her. She talks fast and she is very busy. At that moment I felt she didn't feel the need to spend too much time on our little house. I mean, I'm sure she probably has bigger fish to fry. Gladly, I kept my mouth shut because she quickly reassured us that we could receive whatever listing price we wanted for our home because of our updates, the location and the way homes were selling. We were located down a quaint little dead-end street.

My concern came from the fact that we listed our home several years before and didn't receive very many looks at all. I still felt somewhat discouraged, but decided that I would put it in the Lord's hands and trust Him through Rochelle. She was confident enough for all of us. God brought us this far, may as well trust Him for the rest of it.

The day finally arrived for the photographer to come take pictures of our home. Rochelle called and gave us some instructions and told us that she would be by shortly after the photographer left. I told you she's busy, so she had another appointment. She stays booked and busy.

Shortly after the photographer left, she came by, complimented us on everything, and informed us that she would get the pictures from the photographer the next day. At that point, she would post them to the website and our home would be officially listed to sell. Right before she leaves; it was as if someone grabbed her coattail and called her back. She stopped, turned around, and completely surprised us. She decided that she wanted to take a couple of pictures of her own. When I say a couple, I literally mean two. And she took them with her cell phone. One of the front of the house and one of the backyard. After a few brief words, she left.

The next morning, my husband and I were so excited and could not wait to see the listing of our home and how the pictures turned out. We kept checking the realtor's site and refreshing the page to see if anything was going to come up. Nothing. Finally, something came up! But it's not the pictures from the photographer. The realtor's site posted the two pictures that Rochelle took with her cell phone. One picture of the front and one picture of the back of our house. So, nobody could see all the hard work that we had been doing all this time. My husband had completely redone our bathroom and our kitchen. We had painted, cleared out ALL of our 18 years worth of stuff, and all people could see was the front and backyard of our little house?

Shortly after we saw the pictures, if I remember correctly, she called and told us that she still hadn't received the pictures from the photographer, so she decided to get the ball rolling and went ahead with what she already had; her two pictures. With some degree of disappointment, we said okay and waited to see what would happen next.

Although Rochelle talks fast and is usually in a rush, there is something that feels trustworthy when she speaks. So, we trusted her and the God in her to handle our affairs. About an hour after she posted the pictures, she texted and asked if we could allow a viewing of our home at 1:30 p.m. We said no because our kids were still in virtual school (remember this is during the pandemic) and my husband was still on the clock for work. So, we agreed to 4 p.m. We packed up our German Shepard and left the house.

From that point forward, Rochelle texted us about four different times asking if we would allow viewings of our home hour after hour. Remember, this is only after having posted two pictures of the outside of our house. The last showing was at 8 pm. We finally made it home and settled in. Suddenly, we get a call from Rochelle. We assumed it would be some feedback on what some of the prospective buyers and other realtors had to say about our home. Much to our surprise, our 9:30 p.m. call from Rochelle was actually to inform us that we had an offer! It was above asking, with no contingencies, with an earnest deposit ready to go! Praise God! Can you believe it? Our house was only listed for about an hour with just two pictures showing the outside of the house. And it still ended up with 5 viewings in one day and an above asking offer all in one night! This was absolutely amazing! God is amazing.

Now What

We were so busy trusting God, that we didn't consider giving ourselves a grace period to find our new home. Honestly, our minds were set, that if things worked out as we prayed, we would be able to move right out of our old house and into our new home. I didn't want to move twice, that was one of my prayer requests. I didn't want to move into a smaller place as a layover or go through the trouble of having to put our 18 years worth of things into storage until our next home was available; just to move it all again. But we decided we would leave it in God's hands.

I want to say that it was the next day that we spoke to Rochelle on what our next steps would be. We have got to move quickly on finding our new home, so that we won't be homeless. She calls to inform us that she is about to begin a fast and wants to include us on her prayer list. See what I mean? This is what I'm talking about! This isn't just a job for Rochelle. She wasn't secretive about her relationship with the Lord. She didn't do the cliché saying, " I'll be praying for you". She wanted to know exactly what it was that we wanted, so she could pray about it. She asked us to put together a list of all of our "must-haves" for our new home. My husband and I have had this discussion millions of times throughout the years, so this is the easy part. We agreed on just a few things and sent them to her in our group text. In the meantime, she started taking us to see homes in various locations. We knew we wanted to be closer to the boys' schools and in that general area, but nothing too specific. Well, we didn't think we had any specifics. All of a sudden, God dropped a location down on the inside of me. I knew exactly where I wanted us to look. Instead of sharing this with my husband, I sent a personal text to our realtor. I informed her of how my husband had been so fond of this particular street and that it will be the street I am believing God for. I asked her to privately stand in agreement with me and not to mention it to my husband. The plan was, that after everything is said and done, when we've actually obtained an accepted offer, on the street that we are believing God for; we will show him our text thread and allow him to see that we prayed for this, and here is the manifestation of God's work. She promised to keep this prayer request between us and that was that.

  I need to go back a little bit. We often met with Rochelle. Yes, she was a very busy woman, but she always made time for us. Meetings that were probably only supposed to last 15 minutes or so, would often end after an hour or more. Our relationship had become so much more personable. We quickly became like family and started calling her our aunt. But the time we spent wasn't so business-like that God couldn't be or wasn't a part of it. We prayed together and ministered to one another. Because I had solicited her services and was bold in letting her know that I wanted someone who would believe God with us, she wasn't afraid to let us know if God put something on her heart to say to us. She prophetically stated how she could see where God was going to take us and that it was going to happen quickly. Without thinking, my husband says, " from 0 to 100". She just about jumped out of her seat! "YES!" she said. "It's gonna happen just like that, you watch what I tell you!" Now I'm sure you have figured out where the title of the book came from.

Now, remember, we have accepted an offer on our house. So now we are on the grind when it comes to looking for our next home. Even my youngest son was online finding homes. Rochelle would take us to homes way out in little cities that we were not at all interested in and the prices were way out of our budget. But she said, " I want you all to see the kind of place that God is about to put you in. I know it's not the right location, but it's the style of home and neighborhood". I'm rejoicing on the inside. I know what I had been praying for. And she is speaking right in line with everything I've been praying. Unfortunately, my husband didn't quite know how specific my prayers had been. So, he was trying to enjoy these open houses, but was panicking on the inside all along. LOL. He says he was concerned that I would fall in love with something he couldn't afford. The secret was, I wasn't depending on him for this one. I had talked to God about it before he ever even knew this was going to be a topic.

He That Finds A Wife

I've mentioned my husband a few chapters back, so you kind of know this already. I can mention a thing, and he'll do whatever necessary to obtain it. He simply does not want to tell me "no". It's not that he doesn't trust God. He definitely believes and trusts in the Lord, but he struggles at times, deciding if it's something that he should take on as his own responsibility or if it's something he should wait and trust God for. As his wife, the mother of his children, and his helpmate, I am careful to respect that and not make him uncomfortable in that space.

That's why, as wives, we have to be careful not to add unnecessary pressure on our husbands. Support them. If you have a desire for something that your husband can not provide, you take it to the Lord. Especially if you know that he is doing right and he's doing all that he can to provide. Be careful to not pester your spouse for things that you can live without or things that you can wait patiently for. God will reward you in the end. Be careful of what you say around him. Know that there are times that you will need to know the difference between what he can do and what you're waiting for God to do.

For the most part, my husband functions from his practical side. And I know and respect that. Neither of us grew up rich, so we have always tried to be pretty frugal as adults. In our pillow talk, we have always stressed that we never want to be "house poor" just to look like we have accomplished something. That was the biggest reason that we stayed in our small home for so long.

The market wasn't always as good as it had become during the pandemic. We hadn't always been in position either. Before we married, we agreed that we would base our lifestyle on one income; my husband's. He said I could be a stay-at-home mom and all that. So, that's how we based our decisions. Now that it was time to look for a new home, he's looking at his income and thinking accordingly; which only makes sense. And I was intentional in making sure that he never felt pressured, by me, to rush into doing something that would put us in a compromising situation.

Instead, I would find myself rejoicing with others when they acquired their blessings. About a year or so prior, my sister Rhea had moved into her new home. She had been waiting and praying about a new home for as long as I had. But things worked out for her first. After they moved in, they had us over for a visit. I just couldn't contain myself. I began to rejoice and praise God as if it was my home. I couldn't explain the feeling. I guess I felt like if she received what she wanted, mine had to be on the way. That feeling just brought such joy to me. And even the thought of knowing how long she prayed and waited before she finally received her home; maybe I felt what I thought she felt.

The same thing happened when I went to visit our pastor's new home. I caught Pastor Jackie so off guard that she started recording me because she thought I was trying to be funny. Well, she knew I was serious once my rejoicing turned into tears.

To better explain it, I felt that feeling like my blessing was on the way. I had not received a special Word or a prophecy yet. But my heart was leaping for joy. I had an overwhelming sense of " If I have blessed them with their hearts' desires, I'm going to do the same for you." So, as I rejoiced for them, the Spirit of Joy overcame me. I began praising God in advance for what I knew He had in store for me and my family.

I laugh about it, but in all seriousness, we should rejoice with one another when God is blessing someone. Yours is coming, so start praising Him and making preparations now!

In All Your Doing To Stand, Stand

As we search realtor sites for potential homes, my husband keeps picking out houses that are just blah. While I, on the other hand, keep picking out homes that he keeps raising an eyebrow to. LOL. I say nothing. I keep my faith high and I stay prayed up. I keep trusting that God will reveal to him what He's placing down on the inside of me.

Eventually, Rochelle finds a home in the same neighborhood as the street we want to be on (the street I'm praying for). So, here we are at that point again. Right where I always seem to get to. It's the space of not quite what I asked for, but close enough. Maybe my expectations were too high or my faith wasn't developed to the level I was trying to believe on just yet. The house was located right off the street I wanted to be on. The square footage was just a little less than what we were looking for. It didn't really have a backyard, but it was down a cul de sac. So, at least the boys would have a safe area to ride their bikes like they could at the old house. The master bedroom wasn't on the main level, but the house was move-in ready. I started to compromise everything on my prayer list because time was getting away from us and this was good enough. It was close enough, so it could be good enough; as usual. We had been searching for months. Every time we would find a home of interest, it would receive an offer before we could even get a viewing. And we definitely had a hard time finding anything that held our interest in the boys' school district. So, this house is it.

The home was beautiful. They were asking a little more than we wanted to pay, so we decided to take the time to pray about it and see how God would intervene on our behalf. The house didn't get any other offers and a few weeks had gone by. So, we kept waiting and praying. My husband and youngest son, MaZahn, kept house hunting. They kept showing me house after house until I finally got mad and said, "don't show me anything else! You're messing with my faith. I don't want to be distracted by looking at other houses." So, they stopped showing me; they kept looking though. LOL.

One day, Maddox (my middle son) and I were out and I got a text from my husband. It's a listing. I am instantly irritated. I couldn't get reception at the time, but I'm waiting for a prescription and had to pull over anyway. I'm bored, why not figure out how to open this text. I finally got it to download. It's a listing for a house on the street I've been praying for. I read the description and it meets everything that we put on our list. But it also listed some things that I had prayed about secretly and a few that only my husband knew about. I hadn't said anything to Rochelle because I didn't want to limit her search. To be honest, I guess I felt like my request was a little absurd. Yes, I know He's God, but was I being greedy? So, no. I'll keep that part of my prayer request between God, my husband, and myself. I tell him whatever because we dream together like that.

Anyway, I call my husband almost out of breath! "Did you read the description on the listing you sent me?" He had only seen the basic information. It was on the street he liked, it had the number of bedrooms we wanted, and over the square footage we were looking for. We talk about it and decide instantly that we have to see this house as soon as possible. The next day Rochelle already had us set up to go back to the "almost house". So, we asked her if she could get us a viewing for this new listing we found. She informed us that she already had it lined up. Of course, she did! She knew her assignment and she was on it, okay?

The next day we went to visit the "almost house". We walked around, talked some things through, prayed over the property, and just tried to see what God would say to us. There is a stillness. No answer, no feelings, no nothing. Sometimes it will be that way. Don't be anxious, just wait.

Exceedingly & Abundantly

We left and right up the street is the new listing; the one that's on the street we prayed for. We step in and the house is overflowing with furniture and knick-knacks. But there is still so much space. Every room is huge and filled and it seems like the house never ends. But believe it or not, there is still an upstairs and a basement. This is crazy! We step out onto the breezeway and there is an enclosed gazebo (which is also full of furniture). The whole backyard is fenced in. We're in a neighborhood and the backyard is sitting on half an acre with all of these beautiful mature trees. My mouth is just hanging open (on the inside, of course). I started to get excited, but I wouldn't dare show it.

There were still so many steps that needed to take place. It was great that we actually got to see the house that we wanted to see, but had someone else already put in an offer? Would we be in a bidding war? The market was so competitive right now that if you found a house, you ended up paying tens of thousands more. You had to outbid other people that were fighting for the same home. Things were crazy!

We continued to walk through the home dreaming of what we could do with each space. My husband was starting to show his excitement. He had always loved this neighborhood for some reason. This street, in particular, just really did something for him. So, for this house to be priced within our budget and on his favorite street, he was already sold. Plus it offered a few perks (I won't mention just yet).

Rochelle knew what we wanted. She was excited right along with us. She helped us dream up what we could do with the spaces. She gave her take on how we could repurpose some of the rooms and all the family gatherings we could enjoy. There were so many different things we would be able to do in this home that we hadn't been able to do in our current home.

As we were leaving, another family walked up for their viewing. My heart instantly sank. My husband and I got in the car and started conversing about how we felt about the house. We both loved it. He initially wasn't sure how I felt because I seemed to hold a poker face the entire viewing. I explained how I didn't want to get all excited, just to be let down. It all seemed too good to be true. Were we the first to see the house? Another family came right after us. Would they love it and put in an offer and want to go into a bidding war over the house? I was allowing the enemy to have a foothold in my mind, to be honest. I knew better. I rebuked those thoughts and kept dreaming. We talked about the house all night. The next morning, my husband woke up and said, " I feel like we need to put in an offer today. We need to talk to Rochelle and have her get the paperwork started." And that's what we did.

Chapter 7: The Secret Is Out

Here comes all the tricky stuff. You know the enemy will do things to make you feel like God is not in it, so you'll be discouraged. So, come to find out, the family hasn't lived in the house for the last few years. They have been living in California (3-hour time difference from us). In addition, they are an older, retired, Korean couple. They do not speak fluent English so, everything has to go through their son. He also lives in California, but is a few hours away from his parents. As you can see, this may be a lengthy process. The one good thing is that there was no other offers yet. However, they do still have another viewing scheduled that they were to keep. We made an offer on the weekend and the viewing was scheduled before our offer. That's just how it works, I guess.

In writing this, my memory is not always my strong suit. But I recall us revisiting the dream home again before actually making the offer. This time, we invited Dadda. We always invited him on these types of escapades. He enjoys "window watching" houses, test driving cars, stereos, furniture, whatever. Dadda is definitely the person to take when you want to make a purchase or sightsee. He gets excited with you. He is very informed on most anything. The only problem with him is that he has expensive taste and he expects you to shop like him. He has the go big or go home mentality. And "if you're going to do it, you may as well get the best one they got!" LOL.
Nevertheless, we take him on these types of ventures, anyway.

He keeps it interesting because he enjoys it just as much as we do.

 As we walk through the house again, showing Dadda around, Rochelle makes a call to the owner's realtor. By now, we have made our way outside and are standing on the porch of the house. Dadda can hear some back and forth between Rochelle and the owner's realtor. He asks me what's going on. I inform him that they must have some issues with something and wanted to counter our offer. Dadda immediately goes into spiritual warfare. Yes, he is on the front porch of the house, in this new neighborhood, speaking in tongues loud enough for everybody to hear. I giggle a little and grab his arm and walk him down the driveway to the sidewalk. My husband was already standing down there praying quietly to himself. At that point, we all just began to agree in prayer that things would work out in our favor. Dadda was definitely a prayer warrior. To this day, I attribute a part of us having our home or at least the favor that came with it, to him.

 Rochelle finished her phone call and informed us that they wanted us to come up with $4,000 more. We agreed, Rochelle called their realtor back and insisted that they agree to an acceptance right then. The realtor was able to get an agreement from the son, although he still needed to drive two hours to see his parents. At that point, he and his parents could discuss everything and have them sign the paperwork. Because of his distance from his parents, he would not be able to get the paperwork signed until the weekend. There was a lot of back and forth between our realtors. Rochelle was insistent on making sure that we would walk away with reassurance from their realtor that they would not sell the home from under us. They agreed, so we left with nothing to hold on to for the entire weekend except their word and our faith. You can only imagine how we were feeling. We were still trying to stand in faith and not doubt. Yet, deal with the realization that people are still people and they don't always move according to the way that God instructs them to. Sometimes, money will move people to do things that they would not normally do. I'll just say it that way. And we didn't know who these people were. All we could do was pray and trust God.

    That night, Rochelle secretly texted me a screenshot of my text message to her. She remembered that I asked her to pray for this street. She knew all of our wants and had agreed in prayer with us for it as she helped us on our search. She would frequently send us encouraging text messages, but that night was different. Her heart was so excited because she saw what God had done. We shared our excitement in secret through our messages and waited for the day we could finally reveal our secret to my husband.

    The weekend ended and our offer still stood. Praise God! For some reason, I feel like we had another visit at the house on this particular day. Either way, once I was sure that everything was a go, we were standing in the driveway of our dream home. I gave Rochelle "the look" to let her know that NOW was the time. Rochelle and I could finally show my husband that special text. The one I asked her to stand in agreement with me on about finding our dream home. The prayer was so precise; down to the exact street. He would surely know that we specifically prayed for this because of him. When I showed him the messages, he just dropped and shook his head in disbelief. How amazing is our God?

Do Not Ask Amiss

But now that you know what we prayed for and where we prayed for it to be, let me tell you exactly what my prayer request was.

Let me first say this; we had long outgrown our first home. When it came to entertaining our family and friends, there was never enough space to do so. When the kids would have birthday celebrations, we would have to find a venue or pray vehemently over the weather, so we could host everyone outdoors. We could never host any special occasions or holidays; we just didn't have the space or proper setup to do it. So, it became our prayer that we would have a home large enough to do those things. My husband and I are very close to our families. We didn't like that the burden of entertainment was always on everyone else. Between both of our families, we had the second-largest household.

We had been in our home for so long, we were pretty sure about what we wanted for our next home in order for us to be comfortable and would accommodate all of our needs and desires. My point is, we were not being greedy or asking God for anything that we didn't need in order to flaunt.
In our lengthy period of searching for homes, it became obvious that the more bedrooms a home had, the smaller the rooms would be (unless you have the right amount of square footage). After many open houses, we decided that about 3,000 square feet would be good. I was bent on an all brick home (in my

opinion, brick homes possess a timeless look). We wanted a first floor master and three more bedrooms for our boys to have their own rooms. So, four bedrooms. I had to have an ensuite. I desperately wanted the privacy of my own bathroom. So, at least three bathrooms; ours, the family bath, and a half bath for visitors. I definitely wanted a large kitchen. Naturally, that's the gathering place of most homes and our family is big on holiday cooking. I wanted lots of counter space for my mom, sisters, me, and eventually my grands, to all fit and cook together. We had to have a large family room; our family sits around together often. I wanted there to be enough space for all the family to come together comfortably and not feel cramped. Or if we decided to host something like a birthday gathering, there would be adequate space. We also wanted a three-car garage. Our current home had two and a half. So, we wanted enough space for all of our vehicles to fit and any lawn equipment (unless there was a large enough shed). Now, my husband and I had always bounced around the idea of having a large lot of property. We kind of dismissed that because we figured we would have to live too far from the amenities that we frequent. In addition, we didn't want the high probability of having to have a propane tank, well water, and all that. There were other things that we took on as a priority and decided not to focus on land in our prayer.

    There was this one thing that I never told anyone, besides my husband, that I was praying for. I realized that coming from such a small home and praying ourselves into a large home, furniture would surely be an issue. The only way it wouldn't be is if God was going to come through on one of those ventures that I had been a part of and bless us with a large lump sum of money right when we moved. So, I was bold enough to pray that God would bless us with a fully furnished home. Yes, I asked God to bless us with a house that would be completely furnished. I know it's a big ask, but what's the worst thing that could happen? I also told my husband that whenever we received our dream home, I wanted a piano. Of course, he thought that was ridiculous because I don't even play the piano. I told him that I wanted one because it looks rich to have a beautiful home and a piano. LOL. He said okay, but I could tell "ok" was just to shut me up. He always says I'm "extra", so I think he ignores a lot of what I say and do. He probably figured I would change my mind or forget when the time came. So, although it may be humorous, I feel that there are levels to this. I also believe that God doesn't half step on what He does for us. Meaning, I know that I don't need a piano, but it could very well be a part of the decor if there is ample space. I know that I've seen pianos being given away on web pages like Marketplace, so wanting a piano wasn't a huge ask.

Bringing It All Back

This is where I tell you that when my husband first sent me the listing about our dream home, it stated that the furniture stayed, upon acceptance of the offer. The family only requested to come and remove a few personal items. The day we came to see the house, we walked into a home that was full of beautiful quality furniture. The house was literally overly furnished from front to back; all the way down to patio furniture. It was as if God was trying to be funny. Or maybe He was giving us furniture to choose from. The cherry on top was staring us in the face as we walked through the entrance of the home. It was a beautiful grand piano in the great room (this has to be a joke). The amount of furniture in this house, was the epitome of the scripture Eph. 3:20 (Now unto him who is able to do exceedingly abundantly above all that we ask or think…). I mean, it was like God was trying to be funny just because He knew that I had gone through bouts of doubt. I could almost hear Him say, you better not ever doubt Me again.

We hadn't told Rochelle that furniture was on my prayer list. So, when we walked into the house and told her that the furniture came with the house, she was floored. At that point, my husband then tells her, "I forgot to tell you that a furnished house was on my wife's prayer list." She just squealed and said, "What? You can't make this stuff up!" She actually said that quite often in the time we spent with her. That's just how amazing things were constantly going.

In Due Season

Everything was actually falling into place. After all these years of waiting, God was doing something big this time. It was finally my turn to see Him do the unthinkable in my life.

As fast as they would request information or send something for us to fill out, we would get it done and send it back. Our other prayer request was to be moved in time to host Thanksgiving Dinner for the whole family that particular year. Everything seemed to be working out in our favor until we finally received our closing date. Actually, the closing date would've been fine if the family didn't need the extra time to remove their personal items. This timing was pushing back our timeline. We wouldn't be moved in on time. Besides that, my practical thinking husband is secretly thinking that his family (us) will now be homeless. You can only imagine my conversations with the Lord in that prayer closet.

Father, you said be anxious for nothing, but if this ain't the trying of my faith right now! We know things are being handled behind the scenes. But despite how quickly it felt like we were holding up our end of the bargain, in our eyes, things weren't moving as swiftly as we desired. Nevertheless, we had to keep the faith and keep praising our way through the process.

Faith With Works

The housing market was great for sellers at the time and interest rates on home loans were at an all-time low. This is where the scripture "faith without works is dead" (James 2:20). Not only were we standing in faith, trusting God for what we wanted, but we put in the work of utilizing what we had to handle business. The extra money I received from unemployment could've been used to splurge on foolishness after my immediate bills were paid. Instead, I used what was left to take care of old debt. I helped pay for the updates and repairs on our home and prepared it to be a blessing for a new owner. We got our credit scores together, we did the work, we prepared and positioned ourselves, so when God was ready to do something great, we were ready. I even tithed and gave offerings from my unemployment, for those of you who are unsure if you should or not. It's income and I believe that God is due the first fruits of it. But let's go back to the rates of the housing market. When I say "at an all-time low", I mean interest rates under 3%. We were in position to buy because we kept paying our bills. We could've stopped and taken advantage of all the different forbearances they were giving because of the pandemic. But we ended up qualifying for these great interest rates because we paid off debts on our credit report instead of splurging the extra money.

This is what you call wisdom. Wisdom is using good judgment, having insight, and understanding. You can be wise without having degrees and book smarts. Sometimes, wisdom comes from just listening and being obedient to what God tells you to do.

We don't always understand why God is moving us to do things a certain way. Why were we still feeling compelled to pay bills that we were given an option not to pay? I know it was God giving us that nudge and speaking in our ear that we needed to use wisdom. Pay your bills, double up on some smaller bills, since you have extra money, pay off your debt. Do some updates. We were feeling so accomplished and motivated, not realizing that God was the one putting these desires in us the whole time, to stay on top of handling our business. Another scripture that comes to mind, (Jeremiah 29:11) "I know the plans I have for you, declares the Lord. Plans to prosper you and not to harm you, plans to give you a hope and a future." We don't always have to know what God is doing. But will we trust Him? Will we trust Him enough to take that small step that looks so insignificant? Sometimes it takes that. We have to trust that He knows everything from beginning to end. He has already factored in your inabilities and shortcomings and He doesn't need to tell you the end result before you start taking action. If He says go, just go. The answer may be right around the corner. Then again, it might not. You may not see the answer or result until a long time after. But whenever you sit back and reflect on what He has done, you'll see that He had it all mapped out from the very beginning. We just need to be obedient to see His perfect will be fulfilled. That's what I believe. That was and has been my experience. And now that I have matured in my walk with Him, I try to make my decisions accordingly.

    I am overly emphasizing position because I truly believe that we could've missed one of the biggest blessings of our lives; one that we had been waiting on for years, had we not been in position. This is something that I teach to my children as well. In school, you do your very best, study, act right in class, and pray concerning your subjects. When you give it all you've got and you fall short in an area, that's where the Holy Spirit will kick in and assist you. You can't do half the work, show up late to class, talk when the teacher is teaching, and still expect to excel or expect to find favor. If you do things the right way and maybe your grade in this certain teacher's class is one point away from allowing you to have a 4.0; you could have favor with that teacher, and they could decide to just give you the point. Maybe they could offer you some extra credit to help boost your score because they really like you and want to see you succeed. But if you're the student who "goofs off" and you're a few points away from having a better grade, the teacher will most likely be dismissive of you because they don't think you really care anyway. In other words, you don't have favor with the teacher. It is always best to put your best foot forward. The bible even says, "whatever you do, do it heartily, as unto the Lord and not as unto men, because you know that you will receive an inheritance from the Lord as a reward. It is the Lord Christ you are serving (Colossians 3:23-24)."

I say all this to encourage you to do the work; to do your work. Prepare yourself for God's predestined timing. The fact that we were prepared, put us in a position to receive the best interest rate. The rate we received was unbelievable to everyone in the room when we filled out our final paperwork at closing.

We could have believed God for the home and all that could have worked out, but the interest rate could have still been high. The funny thing is, our interest rate is lower on our new, much larger dream home than it was on our first-time buyer's small home. Crazy, right? But that's what happens when you do things God's way and in His timing. He is so awesome.

Chapter 8: Blessed To Be A Blessing

There was another piece to this story that I failed to mention, but I believe that our blessing would not have been as bountiful had this not happened.

As we began the remodel of our kitchen, I started praying for new appliances. Our stove did not match the other appliances and our dishwasher was probably the smallest size you could possibly buy (but it came with the house) and had stopped working about six months prior.

One day while scrolling through Facebook, a marketplace sale pops up from a friend of ours. What you won't believe is that it's for a stove, a dishwasher & this beautiful hammered copper sink! I knew the quality of this stuff because our friends do pretty well for themselves. Frankly, I didn't even understand why they were remodeling their kitchen (it was so beautiful the way it was). But they had just dropped the price on the items by the time I saw them. So, the price was right up our alley. I showed it to my husband and he urged me to contact them. After speaking with my friend, she gives us all three items for even less than what was listed online! I wanted to cry. God is so awesome!

Long story short, we installed all the newer appliances and got the kitchen all done up! The appliances we received from our friends were worth thousands of dollars, brand new (they were in a new-like condition)! After everyone saw the finished kitchen, they asked, "are you taking those new appliances? I KNOW you're taking that hammered copper sink! That's an expensive sink!" My husband and I agreed that everything stayed. We decided that we were going to put our very best into this home to make it a dream home for the new homeowners. We believed, with all our hearts, that God was going to bless us with our dream home. So, if we made this a dream come true for someone, someone would set up our dream come true for us.

    I said all that to say, be willing to do good and give your best. I believe that if we would have taken those appliances (those three little things that were such a big blessing to us at that moment), we would have missed being blessed with the furnished home that I asked God for. We would have blessed ourselves instead of allowing God to bless us, and instead of us blessing the next person.

    My mind always imagines the drawing of Jesus standing in front of the little girl (you can google it, if you've never seen it before) He is holding one hand out towards her, asking her for the one little stuffed bear she is holding. She is just standing there trying to decide if she should give it to Him. But what she can't see is that He is holding a huge bear, in His other hand, behind His back. She doesn't realize if she would just be willing to give up that one little thing, He has something so much greater. What He has is so great that she will need two hands to hold it. Yet, her mind has her feeling that what she has in her little hands (maybe because her little hands are already full) could not be any better. Logically speaking, how could it be? Her hands are already full. But what she doesn't realize is that our God doesn't just fill your hands. He does exceedingly and abundantly above what you could ask, think or imagine. The bear that God is holding, is so large that she will hardly be able to hold it. How crazy is that? How awesome is that? No matter how much you think you have or have accomplished, God can exceed that, if we just trust Him.

Favor Among Men

    Before we found our dream home, the date for us to move out so our buyer could move in had rolled right on around. So, the week of our move-out date came and we were now in a bind. Now, we had prayed that we wouldn't have to move twice. We've lived in the same home for nearly 18 years. This was going to be a long and tedious process as it was and we didn't have any help. So, we decided since our offer was accepted on our new home and the paperwork was already almost completed, we would ask the homeowners if we could store our things in the new house so we wouldn't have to move them twice. Believe it or not, they said yes! Praise God! This was not the way we saw things happening; we figured God would work out the timing and just let us move into our new home. Instead, we were able to move our things into the new home. But now, what will we do? At this point, we still have almost a month before we can move into our home. So, we speak with our families and work out arrangements to move in with them. We did not want to do this. We knew it would be a tremendous inconvenience for them and us. So, I continued to use my prayer closet to talk to the Lord about what I wanted. And that wasn't it! Nothing was happening; no changes seemed to be taking place. Nevertheless, we praised Him and did what we had to do. Finally, the day comes. We were packing up the biggest U-Haul they had. It was about half full when my oldest son came to me and said, " Mom, someone is reaching out to me on Facebook messenger, but I think that she thinks I'm Dad. I think it's the lady that's buying our house." Confused at what it could be about, I read the message. She was very sweet. She wanted to reach out and thank us for how smoothly the process went and all that. So, we message back and forth for a few minutes until she finds out that we can't move into our new home yet (I won't go into the whole conversation). In the midst of messages, she doubles back and says, "Wait, you can't move yet?" So, I explained a short version of what's happening with our sellers. She instantly says, " Well, I'm not in a hurry. You guys can take your time. I knew that there was a reason I felt led not to terminate my lease." Boy, did I shout! I ran outside to tell my husband as he was loading the truck, "Babe! Our buyer is giving us time to move out! We don't have to move out yet!" He started praising God too! We finished loading what we could live without for the next few weeks and took it to our soon-to-be new home. We were able to call our families and let them know that we didn't need to move in with them.

    Nothing looked like we imagined it would. I honestly feel like God allowed things to take as long as they did, to see if we would trust Him. I mean, He waited until we were packing the truck before we found out our prayer request had been answered. But you know what? We never complained. As much as we didn't like the possibility of being uncomfortable and having to move in with family for a few weeks, we had to continue to thank and praise Him through it all.

    You may say the wrong thing or complain, but when you do, hurry up and repent. Be quick to get it right. Even when you don't feel like it, show God that you know what's right and you're willing to do what's right even when you don't feel like it. He knows your heart anyway. But it shows Him that you're willing to do what it takes to please Him, and He will honor that.

Chapter 9: Do What He Tells You

None of what I have stated is a carbon copy of the way to receive your blessings or answers from the Lord. I am simply giving my testimony and praying that it is a blessing and inspiration to you. I am also not insinuating that anything that God has done for me, was due to my good works, so to speak. I believe in the law of reciprocity, standing on the word, not murmuring and complaining, obedience being better than sacrifice, faith in the impossible, and just simply doing what God puts on my heart to do.

There are so many more stories attached to this blessing that I could write a whole other book. But what I will say is that I know God is still doing the impossible. I am still praying and believing in Him for other things and watching them come to life. He is so good. It's not to say that I haven't had trials, because I definitely have. Some that I care not to mention because I want this to end on a high note.

Stay encouraged knowing that our Father in Heaven cares for you. The scripture I stand on the most is Matt. 6:30," But if God so clothes the grass of the field, which is alive and green today and tomorrow, is cut and thrown into the furnace, will He not much more clothe you?" In other words, why would He care for something as seemingly worthless as grass, but not me or you? He doesn't! And once we realize that, act like that, and stand on that, we will see His Word work in our lives like that.

Before We Were Formed In The Womb

There were certain things that my husband and I discussed pertaining to our dream home; about how we knew God set it aside just for us and stuff like that. And we came up with all these different things about the house that brought those discoveries to light. As I came to a close in writing this book, we spoke about how awesome God is and how we are still in awe of where we are now. Some of the things we brought up were reminders of what we had spoken of before. But we just realized the most amazing thing of all this morning during our pillow talk.

Our dream home was built in 1990. At that time we were about 13 yrs old, which was around the time we met in 8th grade. No sparks just yet, though. We were friends and nothing more at the time.

I'm not sure how long after, but the family before us decided to add an addition to the house. The addition included an extra bedroom, butler's pantry, family room, and a closed-in sunroom that is ultimately a den.

Here's the thing, my husband and I didn't know we would end up together, but God did. Growing up, I always said that I only wanted one child. After conversations with my husband, he expressed that he only wanted one child as well. At least that was how he felt until we had gotten together. I felt that my heart's desire was to have just one child to spoil and give my all love. It wasn't until my husband and I were together, that I desired to have a large family. God knew my heart would change when he and I came together. Only God knew that our children would end up in the school district of our dream home. Funny thing is, one more street over, we would be in a whole different district. Can you believe that? You can't tell me my God ain't good.

Our new neighborhood does not allow fences unless you have a pool, but we have a dog and needed a fenced-in yard. God knew in advance how our life would be set up and that we would, at this very point in our lives, have a dog. In addition to that, the previous homeowners planned to install an inground pool. Well, as we matured and analyzed Michigan weather, we decided that we didn't want the maintenance of a pool when we only have about a good month of heat to even enjoy it. When we did a walk-through of our dream home, we discovered that the yard was fenced (because the neighbors had pools) and because….listen to this! The owner at the time started the project of digging for a pool and stopped. He changed his mind and turned it into a water fountain feature instead. God knew we didn't want a pool. Did he stop building the pool at the point that we started telling God what we wanted?

I can't help but think that this was all being done behind the scenes even as we were teens; before we ever even started dating.

This is the reason that I have learned to be so much more patient when waiting to see God bring my answered prayers into manifestation. I truly believe that there are so many things happening in the background on my behalf. After all this, I'm willing to wait for His perfect will and timing; because in it, I will have what I desire and so much more.

Give It Back

Those of you who know about the process of purchasing a home, know that you have to have an inspection done. Well, we had one and were told that the roof would need to be redone on this almost 4,000 square foot house. We were grateful when he reassured us that we had at least another five years or so before that would be necessary.

We closed and moved into our dream home in November. When December and January came, we were hit with mounds of snow. When it melted, the den began to stream water down the walls. Well, it was freezing cold and the den was technically a closed-in, non-insulated sunroom. So, the water turned into ice. Yes, we literally had ice sickles streaming down the walls of our den. Once the weather was nice enough to melt the snow and even when it rained, we started to have spots where the den would leak and drip water. So much for two more years on the roof. Of course, we had to have someone come out to do some patchwork until we could work out arrangements to have the whole roof redone. But this wasn't going to be a cheap expense. We had been quoted between $25,000-$75,000. Our roof is huge. But the kicker was this; the roofer told us that we would need a new roof before the next winter hit. What?! We just moved! Who has that kind of money? The insurance isn't covering this; the inspector signed paperwork stating that the roof was good for 5-7 more years.

Here goes another thing the Lord and I needed to discuss. My prayer to Him was simply along the lines of reminding Him of His Word. Upon our moving in, we dedicated our home back to the Lord. The significance of doing so, is because our heart's desire is to show Him and remind ourselves that what we have is because of Him. We will use our home to be a blessing to others and to glorify Him in whatever way He instructs us to. In other words, although we live in it, it is His. In the bible it says "the blessing of the Lord enriches and He adds no sorrow (Proverbs 10:22)." Simply put, He adds no trouble to His blessings. I talked to God as I do my earthly father; "Lord, you gave me this as a gift. It is also yours. I know you wouldn't bless me with something and put a burden of this magnitude on us. So, I'm looking for you to take care of this roof. I don't want to take out a loan and have another bill to pay. I want a free roof. Lord, I need you to take care of this."

I kept praising God for our new free roof for the rest of winter, all of spring, and through most of the summer. Then something happened. On our way home, pulling into the driveway, we see some solicitors going door to door. We hurried into the house and shut the door, of course. LOL. Come on, who doesn't? Don't judge me. Anyway, we finally get the dreadful knock at our door. I let my husband answer. The guy does this fast sales pitch about qualifying for a free roof due to possible damage from a hailstorm in our local area a few months ago. All he needs is our name, email, address, and the name of our insurance company. He tells my husband to set up a day for them to come out and they'll let us know if we qualify. We arranged it, they came out, they said we had hail damage and to contact our insurance company. We called the insurance company, they sent their adjuster and the roofing company came, as a representative for us, to look at the same time. Now, it's getting interesting, right? The insurance adjuster can't just ignore what the professional roofer sees. Especially if he's on the roof with him. Before they went up, they informed us that once they finished, it would take a few days to get an answer as to whether or not we qualified for a free roof. So, at this point, I'm in the house speaking in tongues and praying under my breath. We need this free roof.

    My daughter called with a car issue, so my husband left. She had my two oldest boys with her. So, now just my youngest son and I are home waiting for the guys to come down from the roof. They rang the doorbell when they finally finished. I answered, expecting them to give me some follow-up information and to bid me a farewell. Instead, one of the gentlemen says, " well, looks like you qualify for that free roof and…." Before he could say anything else, I hurled over and said, " Wait, what?" He said, " Yep, you'll be getting a new roof, and blah blah…" I don't even remember what he said. I interrupted him, " You just don't know what this means right now. Thank you, LORD!" They smiled and said, "we'll be giving your husband a call to give him all the information as well".

After I closed the door I grabbed my phone and went to our family group chat and Facetimed the whole family. I didn't care that they were together. My husband asked, "what did they say (expecting a summary of what they found and not an answer)." I held the phone up so they could see me dance. I replied, " If He blessed me right here, imma praise Him right here!" I praised and praised until I threw my phone and it turned into an all-out shout. I cried and screamed and praised some more. A free roof?! Yes, a free roof! And the crazy part of it all is that they came to our door, paid our deductible, and did it before winter came.

Another crazy thing that we remembered as the roof was being done; we had received a flyer in the mail about this very opportunity. My husband planned on looking into it, but forgot and ended up losing the flyer. Funny thing is, he found it after they started the work on the roof. It's as if God was chasing us down to bless us.

So, when you see the word dream home mentioned over and over; this is the reason why. No one could ever convince me that this home, this move, this timing, and everything about this situation wasn't divinely set up by my Father God.

Spend Time With Him

I told you about my little tiny cedar closet that I set up as my war room at my old home. It doesn't matter where you pray. God is looking at your heart and your desire to get close to Him. I spent time with Him in that tiny closet until things changed. My situations changed, my circumstances changed, my life changed, I changed. There were so many things that I had grown to be frustrated with within our tiny home. We lived there for so many years and had simply outgrown the space. By the time we were ready to move, I didn't feel any sadness. I was going to miss living so close to our families (because we would walk to their homes in the summer), we could visit at any instance, and even my dad would walk their dogs to our house for exercise and visits. Oh, I was definitely going to miss our "Grand-neighbors" Ron and Dee, but other than that, I was over it.

I hadn't cried or showed any emotion concerning us leaving and moving on to our dream come true. At least not until it came time to do my final check to ensure that everything was cleared out of my prayer closet. The moment I closed the door, tears streamed down my face. My heart filled with all the feelings that I felt when I first started using it. This was the place where my life turned around. This is where I established my true relationship with my Heavenly Father. This is where I learned how to trust Him and stand on His Word. This tiny closet is where He answered one of my biggest prayers. Now, I was leaving it behind.

Walking into my dream home, I now have a whole room right at the entrance. I took pride in my little closet at my old home. Now, God has given me a whole room for me and Him to spend time together in. One day that dawned on me and I just cried and couldn't get it together. In Luke 16:10 it says, "If you can be faithful or trusted with the little things, you will be faithful or trusted with much."

My heart is so full. I constantly think about what He has done and how He was always doing it even when we felt frustrated and stagnant. When we thought nothing was happening and God wasn't hearing our prayers or that we were not worthy. All along, He was orchestrating our lives and positioning everything on our behalf.

Chapter 10:
There Is A Part Two

After everything was said and done; we were moved in and settled. We finally had Rochelle, our realtor (now, "Auntie") come over to our new home to see a few of the updates and changes. We talked a little while as we continued to praise God together over all that He had done. Before she left, she spoke words to us that we will never forget. And whenever we see or speak over the phone, she reminds us of the Word that God gave her for us: "This blessing was only the beginning. There is a part two."

Rochelle Ridgell, I know that we have told you time and time again, but I want to acknowledge you before as many people as I can. Thank you for listening to God. Thank you for being His vessel and shamelessly doing what you do while representing our Heavenly Father. You allowed Him to use you to make our dream home come into manifestation. For that, we will forever be grateful and hold you in our hearts. I continue to pray that you live under an open heaven, that you are continually anointed and graced to do your work, and that you continue to hear the voice of God and see the manifestation of His favor in your life.

In the meantime, we will look forward to our Part II. I can't imagine what God could possibly do next. But after all of this, I trust Him and I welcome whatever He has in store for us.

May your life be forever changed from this day forward as you step out in faith, trust in the Lord, and keep His Word in your heart. I look forward to hearing your testimonies.

Love,
V.V. Hills

Made in the USA
Monee, IL
16 September 2022